LIFE CYCLE OF A...

Butterfly

Revised and Updated

Angela Royston

www.heinemannlibrary.co.uk

Visit our website to find out more information about Heinemann Library books.

To order:

☎ Phone +44 (0) 1865 888066
🖹 Fax +44 (0) 1865 314091
💻 Visit www.heinemannlibrary.co.uk

Heinemann Library is an imprint of Capstone Global Library Limited, a company incorporated in England and Wales having its registered office at 7 Pilgrim Street, London, EC4V 6LB - Registered company number: 6695582

"Heinemann" is a registered trademark of Pearson Education Limited, under licence to Capstone Global Library Limited

Edited by Adrian Vigliano, Harriet Milles, and Diyan Leake
Designed by Kimberly R. Miracle and Tony Miracle
Original illustrations Capstone Global Library Limited 1998, 2009
Illustrated by David Westerfield
Picture research by Tracy Cummins and Healther Mauldin
Originated by Chroma Graphics (Overseas) Pte Ltd
Printed in China by South China Printing Company Ltd

ISBN 978 0 431 99947 0 (hardback)
13 12 11 10 09
10 9 8 7 6 5 4 3 2 1

ISBN 978 0 431 99965 4 (paperback)
13 12 11 10 09
10 9 8 7 6 5 4 3 2 1

British Library Cataloguing in Publication Data
Royston, Angela.
  Life cycle of a butterfly. -- 2nd ed.
  1. Butterflies--Life cycles--Juvenile literature.
  I. Title II. Butterfly
  595.7'89156-dc22

Acknowledgements
We would like to thank the following for permission to reproduce photographs: Dembinsky Photo Association p. 10 (© S. Moody); DRKphoto p. 26 (© Fritz Poelking); Getty Images pp. 13 (© David De Lossy), 16 (© Altrendo Nature), 21 (© George Lepp); Nature Picture Library pp. 17 (© Ingo Arndt), 28 bottom left (© Ingo Arndt); Photolibrary pp. 6 (© Oxford Scientific Films/Breck P. Kent), 7 (© Oxford Scientific Films/J.A.L Cooke), 9 (© Oxford Scientific Films/ Rudie H. Kuiter), 14 (© Oxford Scientific Films/Rudie H. Kuiter), 15 (© Oxford Scientific Films/Rudie H. Kuiter), 19 (© Dan Barba), 20 (© Oxford Scientific Films/Norbert Wu), 23 (© Oxford Scientific Films/Dan Guravich), 24 (© Oxford Scientific Films/J.A.L Cooke), 25 (© Oxford Scientific Films/J.A.L Cooke), 27 (© Brian Kenney), 28 top left (© Oxford Scientific Films/J.A.L Cooke), 28 bottom left (© Oxford Scientific Films/Rudie H. Kuiter), 29 top right (© Oxford Scientific Films/J.A.L Cooke), 29 bottom (© Oxford Scientific Films/J.A.L Cooke), Photoshot p. 22 (© NHPA/ Dr Eckart Pott); Shutterstock pp. 4 (© Leighton Photography and Imaging), 5 (© GJS), 8 (© Lori Skelton), 11 (© sjgh), 12 (© Cathy Keifer), 18 (© Lori Skelton), 28 top right (© Lori Skelton), 29 top left (© GJS).

Cover photograph reproduced with permission of Minden Pictures (© Michael Durham).

We would like to thank Michael Bright for his invaluable help in the preparation of this book.

Every effort has been made to contact copyright holders of material reproduced in this book. Any omissions will be rectified in subsequent printings if notice is given to the publisher.

Contents

Some words are shown in bold, **like this**. You can find out what they mean by looking in the glossary.

What is a butterfly?

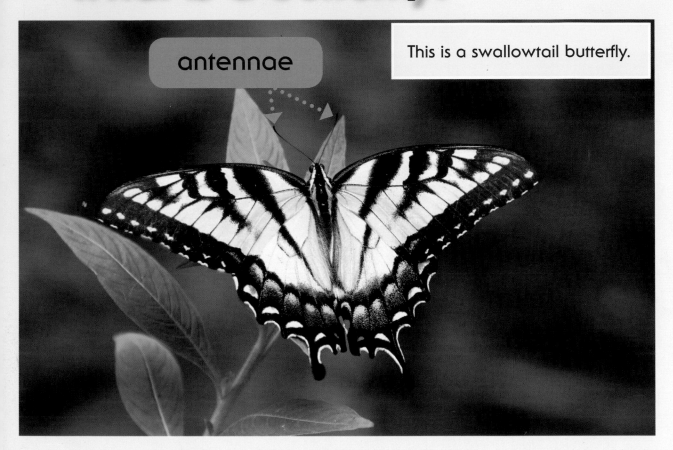

antennae

This is a swallowtail butterfly.

A butterfly is an **insect**. It has six legs, four wings, and two **antennae**. Many butterflies have brightly coloured wings.

| 1 day | 1 week | 4 weeks | 6 weeks |

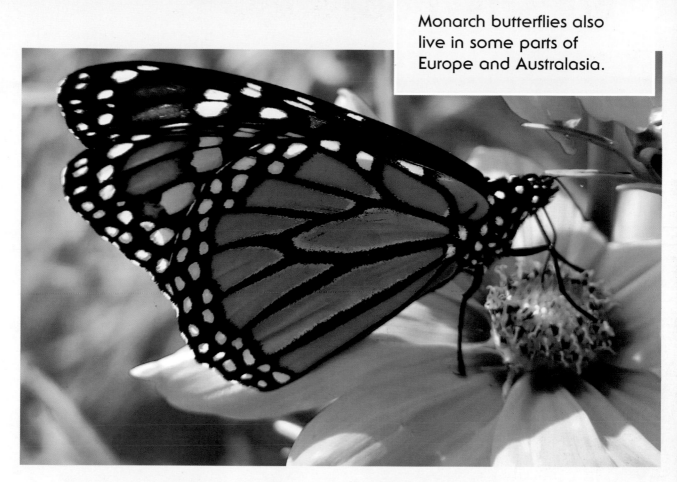

Monarch butterflies also live in some parts of Europe and Australasia.

Many kinds of butterflies live in different parts of the world. The butterfly in this book is a monarch butterfly from North America.

10 weeks

32 weeks

32 weeks

Butterfly eggs

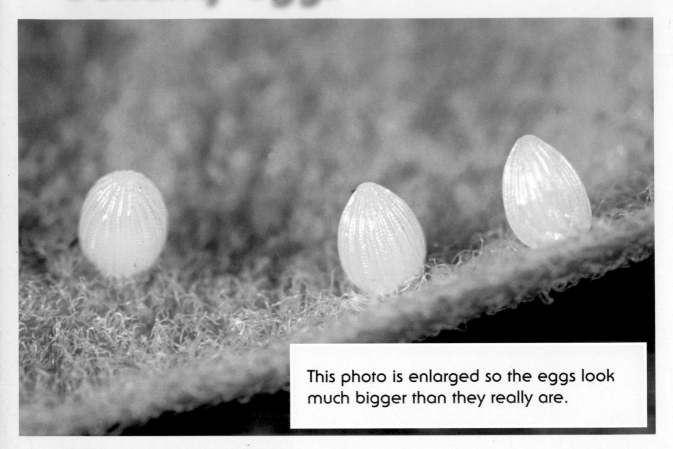

This photo is enlarged so the eggs look much bigger than they really are.

Every butterfly begins life as an egg the size of a pinhead. The monarch butterfly lays her eggs on a **milkweed** leaf.

1 day

1 week

4 weeks

6 weeks

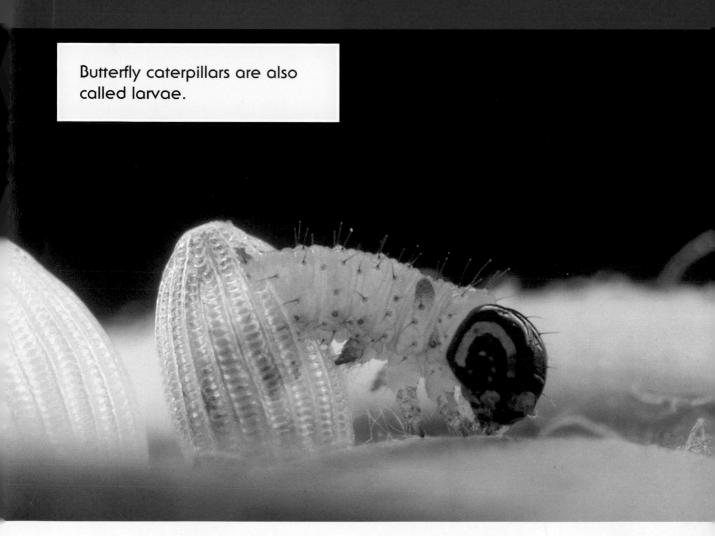

Butterfly caterpillars are also called larvae.

Just over a week later, the eggs begin to **hatch**. A small **caterpillar** crawls out of an egg! It ate a hole in the egg and now it will eat the eggshell.

10 weeks

32 weeks

32 weeks

A few days later

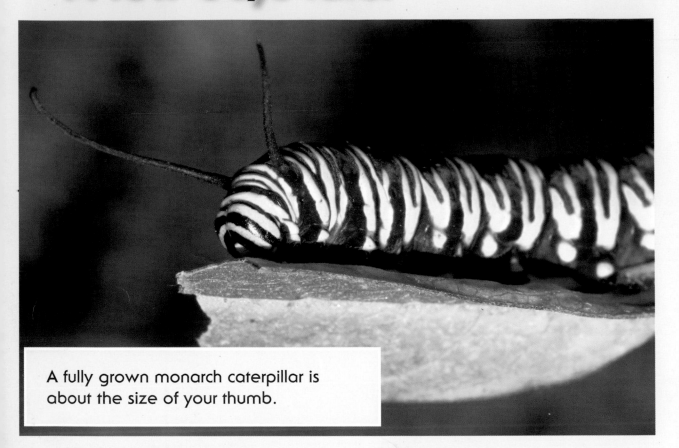

A fully grown monarch caterpillar is about the size of your thumb.

The **caterpillar** eats and grows bigger. It chews through a **milkweed** leaf with its strong **jaws**. Soon it has eaten a big hole in the leaf.

Caterpillars chew using sharp, teeth-like points.

All the eggs have **hatched** and many monarch caterpillars are feeding on the milkweed plant. They crawl from leaf to leaf, eating as they go.

10 weeks

32 weeks

32 weeks

1 week

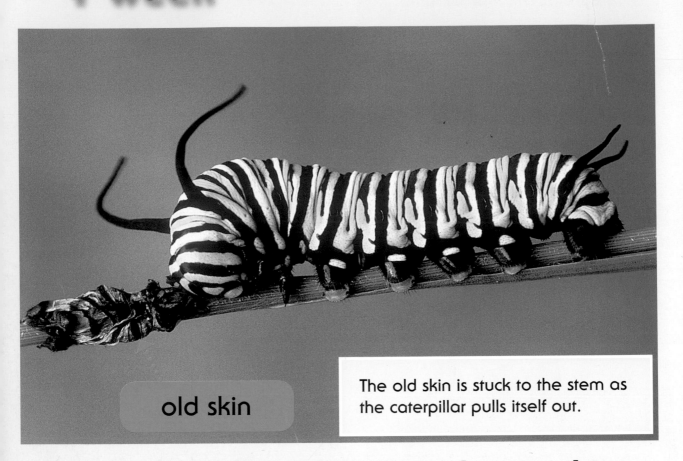

old skin

The old skin is stuck to the stem as the caterpillar pulls itself out.

The **caterpillar** is growing, but its skin is not. One day its skin is so tight it splits open. The caterpillar has a new and bigger skin underneath.

1 day | 1 week | 4 weeks | 6 weeks

The stems on this milkweed plant are covered with hairs.

The caterpillar will shed its skin four times as it grows. It crawls away, clinging to the **milkweed** plant with its many legs.

10 weeks

32 weeks

32 weeks

2 weeks

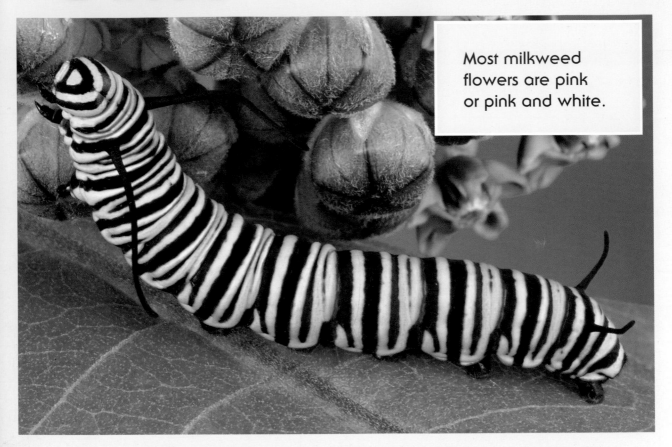

Most milkweed flowers are pink or pink and white.

The **caterpillar** eats and grows. Other animals do not eat it. **Milkweed** leaves have something in them that makes the caterpillar taste nasty.

1 day   1 week   4 weeks   6 weeks

This bird catches insects to feed its young.

Many birds catch **insects**, but they leave the monarch caterpillar alone. They have learned that the monarch tastes nasty.

10 weeks

32 weeks

32 weeks

4 weeks

The **caterpillar** is fully grown. It makes a silky pad on a leaf and grasps it. The caterpillar's stripy skin splits for the last time.

Caterpillars hang from the leaf when their skin splits for the last time.

Underneath the skin is a green **pupa**. The caterpillar is ready to change into a butterfly!

A pupa is also called a chrysalis.

6 weeks

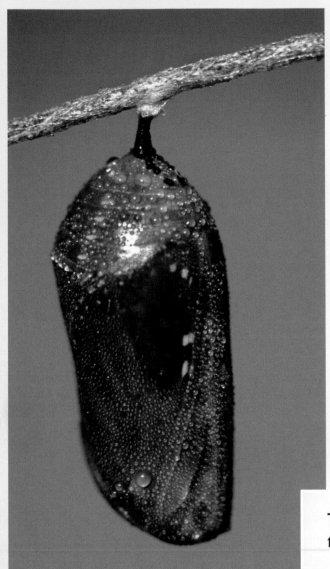

Inside the hard shell of the **pupa**, the **caterpillar**'s body changes. Then the pupa cracks open and the butterfly pulls itself free.

The pupa takes a few hours to get hard and dry.

1 day

1 week

4 weeks

6 weeks

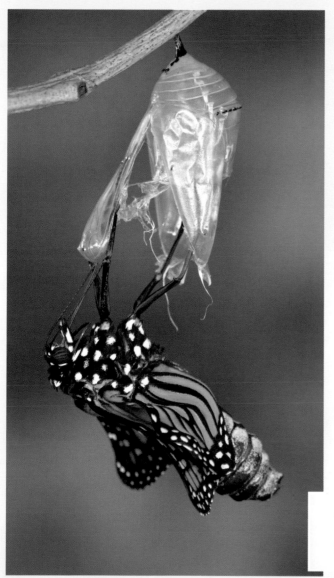

At first the butterfly's wings are damp and crumpled. As the wings dry, they slowly open. The butterfly is ready to fly away.

The butterfly grows in the pupa for 10 to 14 days.

10 weeks

32 weeks

32 weeks

8 weeks

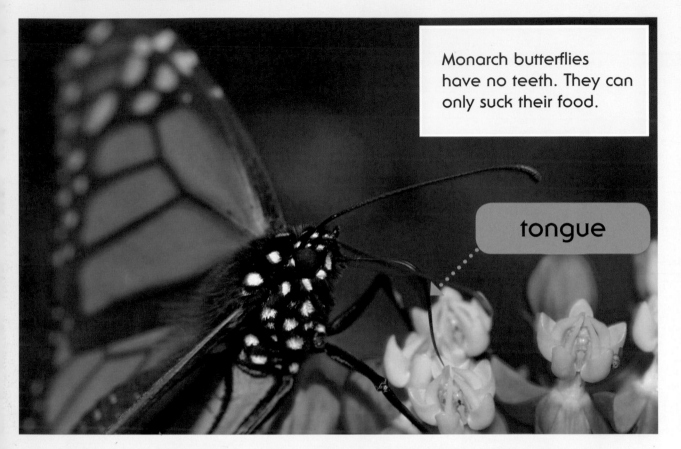

Monarch butterflies have no teeth. They can only suck their food.

tongue

The butterfly flies from flower to flower. It unrolls its long tongue and sucks up the sweet **nectar** in the flowers.

1 day

1 week

4 weeks

6 weeks

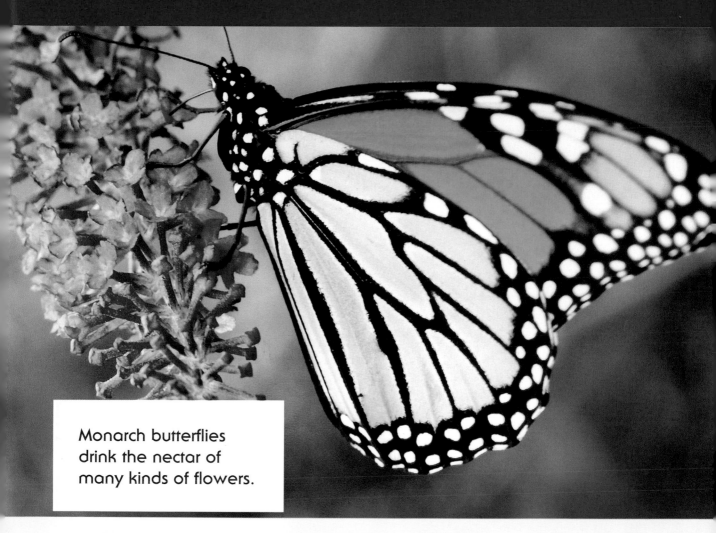

Monarch butterflies drink the nectar of many kinds of flowers.

Birds do not try to catch the butterfly. It still has the nasty taste that the **caterpillar** had.

10 weeks

32 weeks

32 weeks

10 weeks

It is autumn. Short days and colder weather let monarch butterflies know it is time go to a warmer place.

The monarch butterflies gather together on the branches of trees.

1 day	1 week	4 weeks	6 weeks

Monarch butterflies in the west of North America fly to southern California.

Suddenly they all flutter up into the sky. They fly south until they reach the mountains of Mexico. The weather there is warm even in winter.

10 weeks

32 weeks

32 weeks

14–30 weeks

Gathering together helps monarchs keep warm.

The butterflies are very tired when they get to Mexico. They gather on a pine tree to rest.

1 day

1 week

4 weeks

6 weeks

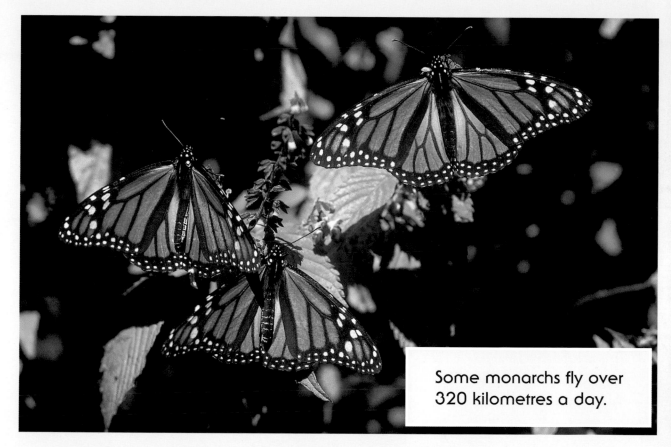

Some monarchs fly over
320 kilometres a day.

When spring comes, the sun warms
the butterflies. They feed from
flowers. Most of the butterflies start
to fly north.

10 weeks

32 weeks

32 weeks

32 weeks

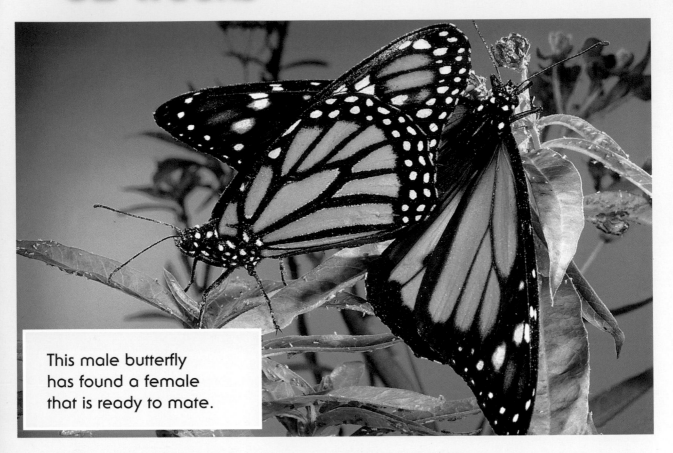

This male butterfly has found a female that is ready to mate.

The butterflies rest during the journey. The male butterflies find females that are ready to **mate**. After mating, the females lay their eggs.

1 day	1 week	4 weeks	6 weeks

eggs

Females lay their eggs on the undersides of milkweed leaves.

They lay them on a **milkweed** plant. The butterflies live only for a few more weeks.

10 weeks

32 weeks

32 weeks

The journey continues

Snow and storms can kill monarchs.

Back in Mexico, some butterflies have been battered by a big storm. Some recover and will fly north. Others will die on the journey.

| 1 day | 1 week | 4 weeks | 6 weeks |

The eggshell is the caterpillar's first meal.

Along the way, **caterpillars** are **hatching**. When they change into butterflies they will fly north. There they will **mate** and lay eggs of their own.

10 weeks

32 weeks

32 weeks

Life cycle

Egg hatching

1 week

4 weeks

6 weeks

10 weeks

32 weeks

32 weeks

Fact file

- The wings of a monarch butterfly are about 10 centimetres (4 inches) across. This is nearly as wide as your hand span.

- Monarchs fly further than any other kind of butterfly. During their long journeys north and south they fly up to 3,000 kilometres (1,865 miles).

- Butterflies use their **antennae** to smell and to feel. They smell food and the special chemicals a male monarch gives off when he is trying to **mate**.

- In one day, a **caterpillar** may eat many times its own weight in **milkweed** leaves.

Glossary

antennae feelers on an insect's head

caterpillar young butterfly or moth before it changes into a pupa

hatch break egg so that a young caterpillar can come out of it

insect very small animal that has six legs, four wings, and three parts to its body

jaws the moving parts of a caterpillar's mouth

mate come together (a male and a female) to produce young

milkweed the plant that monarch caterpillars eat

nectar sweet juice in some flowers

pupa stage in life when a caterpillar changes into a butterfly or moth

More books to read

From Caterpillar to Butterfly (How Living Things Grow), Anita Ganeri (Heinemann Library, 2007)

Insects (Animal Young), Rod Theodorou (Heinemann Library, 2007)

The Life of a Butterfly, Clare Hibbert (Raintree, 2004)

Index